Lessons from Our Living Past

edited by JULES HARLOW

ASSOCIATE EDITORS
Kelly Cherry

Seymour Rossel

Carol Sanders

EDUCATIONAL CONSULTANT
Pearl Zeitz

Illustrated by Erika Weihs

Lessons from Our Living Past

BEHRMAN HOUSE, INC. Publishers
New York, N.Y.

Second printing, 1978

The story *The Wind and I* is used with the
permission of Schocken Books Inc.

© Copyright 1972, by Behrman House, Inc.
1261 Broadway, New York, N.Y.

MANUFACTURED IN THE UNITED STATES OF AMERICA
Library of Congress Catalog Card Number: 72-2055
ISBN 0-87441-085-1

10 9 8 7 6 5 4

For Parents and Teachers

To a greater or lesser degree, every civilization idealizes its past. In our own country, for example, children learn in school of a republic established by men imbued with the highest moral purpose and bent upon giving universal social and political form to an abstract principle of individual liberty; or of a civil war waged nobly by two foes, the one struggling to vindicate a principle of human equality, the other to defend a proud and cultivated way of life. These visions of history, which are essentially mythological in nature, contain a large measure of distortion, but an equally large measure of truth: ideal truth. Viewed through the lens of mythology, the actual events and figures of history assume inflated proportions; as if at the necessary bidding of society itself, they undergo a crucial and far-ranging fictionalization. Men in the mythic vision become heroes, perfect and whole in their character, altogether consistent in behavior—and in nothing more consistent or more perfect than in their unyielding devotion to inflexible principle. Events themselves, shedding the skin of circumstance and accident, stand forth in their boldest and most compelling aspect: they become turning points, inevitable, unique, laden with significance, prefigurative of the future course of history. But if inflation is one characteristic of the mythologizing impulse, simplification is another. The great myths and legends do not on the whole concern themselves with complexities of human motivation —with the shades and nuances of individual personality, the subtle maneuvers of the spirit and the discriminating actions of consciousness. They tell a simple, if grandiose, tale.

Mythology, then, is the conscious effort to recreate the past as a model, and a civilization stamps itself uniquely and for all time in accordance with the particular models it chooses to enshrine and celebrate in its legends. In the mythological literature of the West, the models settled upon have frequently been the fixed virtues of character, as in the great epic poems that strive to illustrate, through the dramatic tale of a hero's adventures, those qualities which the culture holds most dear: the cunning of Odysseus, for instance, or the fortitude of Aeneas, the constancy of Lancelot or the valor of Roland at Roncevaux. In each case the quality is regarded as inseparable from the legendary hero who embodies and exemplifies it and whose character, considerably larger than life, dominates the epic narrative as a whole. The hero and the virtue he typifies, one and inseparable, constitute the mythic model.

In several critical respects the models offered by the myths and legends of the Jewish people differ from this norm, and the differences themselves tell us much about the specific values of Judaism. Rather than as figures of superhuman proportions, the principals of Jewish legend—even of those legends based directly on the heroic narratives of the Bible—appear to us in the common garb of humanity; whereas the epic hero is larger than life, the "hero" of Jewish legend is precisely life-sized. Furthermore, what the typical Jewish legend strives to inculcate is not a specific trait of character, an inner disposition or abstract virtue, but rather a pattern of ideal human behavior; emphasis is laid on strategies of action rather than on the cultivation of a given quality of spirit. At the heart of these divergencies, as we might expect, lies a distinction of value. The moral world of the epic poem is self-contained and self-referring. It is the hero alone who defines the behavior which marks him, in turn, as a human paragon; apart from him, the model does not exist. Jewish myth, by contrast, insists on a standard of judgment beyond the narrative frame, in the body of revealed truth that is the law and faith of Israel; the model exists only with reference to that standard. While the epic encourages us to identify spiritual excellence with a particular figure and with the heroic qualities he displays, Jewish legend encourages us to recognize and esteem those elements of behavior that most closely resemble the ideals embodied in Jewish law; to this exercise considerations of person and of attitude are finally irrelevant.

Such differences aside, however, all myth may be said to share a common purpose. In offering an idealized version of the past, accompanied often enough by a large measure of the wishful and the imaginary, by improbable juxtapositions of time and place and by fanciful characterization, it conveys a species of truth which no "objective" account of reality can match. Mythological truth is not the same as historical truth, which is infinitely more complicated and brutal. Nor is it the same as abstract truth, the truth of philosophy and of religion. Mythology tells us the truth about ourselves by reminding us of the moral possibilities of our own lives, and it does so by giving us the events and figures of our past as models of perfection. Its truth is injunctive, holding out the hope of moral advancement, and investing us with the urge to create a future worthy of such models, of such a past.

J. H.
New York City
Tammuz 5732

Contents

1

Who Will Be My Surety?

Introduction

A surety is something you give in return for something else. When people agree to be friends, they promise to be loyal to one another, and they often exchange gifts with one another. Sometimes a solemn agreement of friendship is called a covenant.

The Jewish people made a covenant with God at Mount Sinai, and in return for the gift of the Torah, they offered their children as surety.

The first story we will read this year tells why God thought this was a fair trade. It also tells us what the Jews meant when they gave Him their children.

Story

When Moses went up Mount Sinai to speak with the Lord, the people of Israel waited below for him to return.

The people of Israel were very anxious. They wondered what the Lord would say to Moses. Then they saw Moses coming down the mountain. They turned to him eagerly and, as they looked at his face, they saw that he was sad.

"What has happened?" they asked him.

Moses spoke to them and said, "The Lord wishes to give us a most wonderful gift, a precious thing."

Excitedly, the people asked, "What is this gift?"

"It is called the Torah," Moses said. "In its words the light of truth shines like pearls in the dark seas. In the Torah there are stories which teach us how God wishes us to live.

"There are laws in it also, laws which teach us how to live peacefully with our neighbors so that a man will love his fellow men. The Torah will teach us how to live as free men, so that we will never be slaves again."

The people remembered Egypt where they were slaves of the Pharaoh. They did not wish to be slaves again. They wanted to be free. They wished to live in peace. Truly, they thought, God's Torah is a great gift.

But Moses was still sad.

"Why are you unhappy, Moses?" the people asked.

Moses sat upon a rock at the foot of the mountain. "God will not give us this gift of Torah unless we promise Him something in return. We must offer him a surety."

Then the people too were sad. "What have we to offer in exchange for such a precious gift?" one man asked another. "A gift like this is worth empires, and we are a poor people in the desert. Now we will never have the gift of Torah."

But the women of Israel came to Moses and said, "We have bracelets with rubies and rings with diamonds. We have precious necklaces and pins. We will give them all to the Lord in exchange for the Torah."

So Moses went up the mountain again and spoke with the Lord. But when he returned, he was still sad.

"The Lord has said that His Torah is more precious than all the rubies and diamonds in the world. The Torah is so bright that it will light the souls of men. Not even a thousand diamonds can do that!"

Then the people sat on the sand of the desert and thought.

All night long the people thought, and when the sun came up they had an idea. "We will offer the Lord our great leaders, Moses and Aaron, as surety for the Torah. Surely the Lord will accept the loyalty of Moses and Aaron in exchange for His wonderful gift."

So Moses went up Mount Sinai to the Lord again. But again he was sad when he returned.

"The Lord has spoken and told me that He cannot accept Moses and Aaron as surety. They are already His; they have already pledged their loyalty to the Lord."

Now in the camp of the Israelites there was an old man whose wisdom was very great. When this wise man heard Moses' words, he rose and spoke to the people.

"God has offered us *His* most precious possession, the Torah. Now we must offer God *our* most precious possession. If a man could choose only one thing in all the world to be his own, would he choose precious jewels? No. Would he choose an honored leader? No. Would he choose money? No. What would he choose if he had only one choice?—his children!"

Then the people turned to Moses. "Yes!" they cried out. "We will offer our children as surety for the Torah. If God will give us His Torah, we will teach it faithfully to our children. And our children will teach it to their children. What could be a better surety?"

So Moses went up the mountain again to speak with the Lord. And when he came down, he was carrying the Tablets of the Law, the Torah which God had given him.

Moses stood before all the people of Israel and said, "The Lord has given us the Torah. Our children will be His surety. For the Lord has said that all men are His children, and the children of all men are precious to Him."

Then the people of Israel thanked the Lord by studying His Torah, and they have kept their promise by teaching the Torah to their children from that day until this.

Questions

1 What is a covenant? Have you ever heard of the American Indian ceremony of "blood brothers"?

2 How is a covenant with God different from a promise to be loyal to a friend?

3 What is a surety?

4 What did the Israelites offer first as surety for the Torah? Was one of the offerings generous? Was one rather silly? Why?

5 Since you are the ones who have inherited the Torah, what do you think of the idea of studying it?

Akiva and the Rock

Introduction

A grown man who can neither read nor write becomes a famous rabbi. How? Through perseverance: *stick-to-it-iveness. Once Akiva learns from Rachel that it is never too late to begin, he works away at his task like water wearing away stone, slowly, steadily, drop by drop, letter by letter.*

Story

Once there was a poor peasant named Akiva who could neither read nor write. The only thing he knew how to do was to herd sheep, and so he became a shepherd for a wealthy man named Kalba Savua. All day he watched the sheep grazing, and at night he slept in the stable.

Now Kalba Savua had a young daughter named Rachel, who was both beautiful and bright, gracious and good. Akiva gazed at her longingly every day, wishing he could speak to her and tell her that he loved her. But he was only an ignorant shepherd; what would she want with a simpleton like him?

16

One afternoon Rachel noticed Akiva as he was driving the flock out to pasture. "Shepherd lad, come and talk to me," she called. Akiva answered bashfully; he was ashamed of his rough speech. But Rachel encouraged him and soon the two were deep in conversation. Rachel saw that in spite of his lack of learning, Akiva had a quick mind and knew many things not found in books.

"Where did you learn so many interesting things?" she asked him.

"From the fields and the river, from the birds and the animals," he replied.

"Imagine how wise you would be if you knew Torah too!" she exclaimed.

From then on, Akiva saw Rachel every day, and little by little she fell in love with him, for she saw that he was good and clever in spite of his ignorance.

When Rachel married Akiva, Kalba Savua was very angry, and he disinherited her. But Rachel was content to live in poverty with her shepherd husband.

Akiva and Rachel were very happy, except for one thing. Akiva was ashamed that he was un-educated, and Rachel was sad that her husband did not know Torah.

Akiva sighed, "I am already a grown man and I still do not know how to read. I cannot tell an *aleph* from a *bet* and I do not know a word of the Torah."

"But you are not too old to study," Rachel said. "No one is ever too old to study."

But Akiva shook his head. Really, he wished to learn the Torah. He wished it with all his heart. But he did not think that he could.

One day Akiva was walking in the woods, alone and downcast, when he passed a rushing stream. A huge granite boulder lay in the stream. In the middle of the boulder was a large hole, through which the water bubbled and flowed.

Akiva stared at the rock in fascination. "How wonderful," he murmured. He realized that tiny drops of water, beating for many years against the rock, had carved that hole in the stony granite.

"If drops of water can carve a hole in hard rock," said Akiva to himself, "then the words of the Torah can pierce their way into my hard head." And that very day, with his wife's blessing, he left for the city to enter a house of study. His instruction began at the beginning: the letter *aleph*.

Years later Akiva returned from his studies, a famous rabbi. Rachel had patiently waited for him throughout the long years. Kalba Savua and all the townspeople came to pay their respects to the great rabbi who was famous for his wisdom. Then Rabbi Akiva called Rachel to his side and said, "If it were not for Rachel's desire for me to study, and for her patience in waiting long years for my return, I could not have persevered in my studies. Rachel must share in the respect you pay me."

Questions

1 Why did Rachel want Akiva to study?

2 Do you think it is easy to *begin* to study when you are already grown up?

3 What does the word *perseverance* mean? Who persevered?

4 In which ways did Rachel and Akiva each persevere?

The Fox and the Fish

3

Introduction

Here we have a fable, a story that is really two-stories-in-one. First, this is the story of a fish who outwitted a fox; but at the same time, it is the story of Rabbi Akiva and why he kept on studying the Torah even after the Romans outlawed it.

See if you can tell how the story about the fish is like the story about the rabbi.

Story

In the time of Rabbi Akiva, the Romans who ruled over Palestine ordered the Jews to stop studying the Torah or be put to death. But Rabbi Akiva would not stop studying. One day a nonbeliever came to him and asked, "Rabbi, why do you risk your life by studying and teaching the Torah? Why don't you follow the Roman rules, live as they do, and be safe?"

Akiva answered with one of his favorite stories:

There once was a fox who had gone hungry all day. Rabbits had run too quickly for him, and

squirrels had hidden before he could trap them with his heavy paw. Now the afternoon sun was making him tired and lazy. If only he could find something to eat and a place in the shade to rest. That was when he thought of the stream.

It was a small stream, filled with swiftly swimming fish, and now, as the hungry fox approached it, he began to think of ways to get one of the fish to swim close enough to catch. If you only use your head, he thought, you can outsmart almost any creature. The fox thought he was very smart indeed.

When the fox came to the edge of the river, he sat very still on the edge of the bank and let his tongue hang out of his mouth like a tired dog. An old fish came slowly swimming past and paused to look at the panting fox.

"What is happening in the forest?" the old fish asked.

"Come closer," said the fox. "Come closer to the shore and I will tell you what I have seen and why I have run all this way."

The old fish swam a little closer to hear the sly fox's whispering voice.

"Men have come into the forest," said the fox in a soft voice, moving his paw closer to the fish. "Some are heading toward the stream, carrying nets to catch you!" The fox lowered his voice even more, so that the old fish had to come closer still to the water's edge to hear his words.

"The fishermen are looking for a nice, fat fish like you. But they will not hunt for a fox, because we are too skinny and our meat is tough to eat."

The fox raised his paw to point at the silver fish.

"So I have come to help you, my friend. Climb out of the water and onto my back. I will carry you to safety where the fishermen will never find you."

The fox licked his lips and looked at the fish. Then he leaned over a little and dipped his paw into the water, to scoop up the silver fish.

But the fish had moved so that the fox only splashed water on himself with his paw.

"Aren't you coming?" asked the fox, shaking the water off his sleek fur.

"No, indeed," said the silver fish. "A fish out of water will die without any doubt. But as long as I am in the water, I can try to avoid the fisherman's net—and the fox's paw too."

Now, when Rabbi Akiva had finished telling the story of the fox and the fish, he added this: The Torah is a Jew's home, just as the water is a home for fish. Without the Torah, a Jew is like a fish out of water. If we are in danger even now while we study Torah, how much greater will be our danger if we leave our studies?

Then Rabbi Akiva went back to his studies.

Questions

1   Why do you think the Romans wanted to stop the Jews from studying Torah?

2   What connection was there between the fish's problem and Akiva's problem? Is there a connection between the two answers?

3   What does the phrase "like a fish out of water" mean?

4   Is there any place in the world today where Jews are not permitted to study Torah? What is happening there?

Hillel's Great Rule

4

Introduction

Ethics is the study of what is right and what is wrong. In this story, a stranger visits two great rabbis and asks to be taught Torah while standing on one foot. The first rabbi turns him away. The second teaches him a great ethical rule.

Story

In Jerusalem many years ago there were two great teachers, Hillel and Shammai. Each had his own school. They were not big schools with many teachers, but were small, and stuffed with books, with chairs and with tables. Part of the day the students studied all by themselves and part of the day the teachers would speak to them, teach them, and tell them stories.

It happened that a non-Jew came to the school of Shammai and asked to see the teacher. Shammai was speaking to his students at the time and the doorkeeper interrupted him at a very important point. Shammai came to the gate and saw the non-Jew standing on one foot.

"What are you doing?" Shammai demanded.

"I have come to learn the Torah," said the non-Jew. "Teach it to me while I stand on one foot."

"You are crazy," said Shammai. "First you come and interrupt my lessons. Then you ask me to do a thing which cannot be done. Many wise men spend their whole lives studying the Torah, learning all the rules and all the thoughts which men have had about the rules. Can I teach all of that to you while you stand on one foot? Now go, do not bother me further, unless you wish to be serious."

The non-Jew saw that Shammai was angry, and he went away.

At the school of Hillel, the non-Jew found no doorkeeper at the gate. He tried the latch and found it open, so he went inside. The school of Hillel was a single room. Books were in shelves on every side of the room and students sat studying quietly. The non-Jew came to the door and called into the room, "Is the teacher, Hillel, here?"

"He is here," said a student, looking up from the book he was studying.

A short man came to the door and blinked in the bright sunlight. "I am Hillel," he said.

Then the non-Jew raised one leg up as he had done before at the school of Shammai. "Now," he said, "I have come to study the Torah. Teach it to me while I stand upon one foot."

25

Hillel was silent. He knew that it was a difficult request. All his life Hillel had studied the Torah and now he taught many students. Yet even though he was a great teacher, he still did not know everything about the Torah. He looked at the non-Jew tottering on one foot and waiting in the bright afternoon sun for his answer.

Finally, Hillel spoke. "Do not unto others what you would not have them do unto you. That is the Torah; all the rest is commentary. Now put your foot down, and go and study."

"Yes," said the non-Jew. "I will study with you."

Questions

1   What did the non-Jew mean when he said, "Teach me Torah while I stand on one foot"?

2   What is Hillel's Great Rule? What makes it *great*? How does it teach us what is *ethical,* what is right and what is wrong?

3   Why did Hillel add, "Now, go and study"?

4   Why did the non-Jew say he would like to study with Hillel?

5 Abraham Argues With God

Introduction

Sodom and Gomorrah were two cities that God destroyed long ago, on account of their wickedness. Before He destroyed them, He told Abraham what He planned to do. Abraham wanted to make sure that God would not fail to be both just and merciful. Our story today is the story of this conversation between Abraham and God.

Story

When the Lord saw the evil of Sodom and Gomorrah, the cities of the plain, He said, "I will destroy these two cities and all the people in them. But because I have promised Abraham the land and all that is in it, I will first tell Abraham."

The Lord came to Abraham and said, "Abraham, the time has come and I must destroy Sodom and Gomorrah. For fifty-two years I have warned them by making the earth tremble and the ground shake. But they have not listened to My warning and they are evil."

Then Abraham said, "Is this the way of the

Lord? Does God destroy the bad men and the good men with them? If there are fifty good men in Sodom and Gomorrah, would You not save the cities for the sake of the fifty men?"

The Lord said, "For the sake of fifty good men, I will save the cities of the plain."

Abraham spoke, "And if there are only forty-and-five good men, will the Lord who created heaven and earth destroy the cities because only five of the fifty are missing?"

The Lord said, "I will not destroy the cities if I find forty-and-five good men."

Abraham spoke again, "And if there are forty good men. Would You destroy the cities if forty good men are in them?"

The Lord said, "I will save the cities for the sake of the forty."

Then Abraham bowed low before the Lord. "Let not the Lord be angry. What if there are only thirty good men? Surely, the Lord will also save the cities for the sake of thirty?"

The Lord spoke and said, "Even for the sake of thirty good men, I will save Sodom and Gomorrah."

"And for the sake of twenty good men?" Abraham asked.

"Even for the sake of twenty I will save the cities," God answered.

Then Abraham spoke once more. "Let not the Lord be angry, for I speak only this once and I will not speak again. What if there are ten good men in both cities. Will the Lord who made man in His image destroy the cities of Sodom and Gomorrah if there are ten men within them who are good?"

The Lord spoke, "If ten good men may be found in Sodom and Gomorrah, I will save the cities for the sake of ten."

Then Abraham spoke no more.

But in all of Sodom and Gomorrah there were not ten good men, and God destroyed the wicked cities. And God did not forget the words of Abraham; He did not destroy the good men with the bad men.

So it was that Lot and his family, who lived in the city of Sodom, and who obeyed the laws of God, were saved when God destroyed the city.

Questions

1 Abraham protested to God that He should not kill the good people with the bad people. Is protest good?

2 There are lots of protests going on today. Can you think of some?

3 There are two ways to protest. What are they? Is there a time for each?

4 Did Abraham protest in a respectful way?

5 Was God reasonable?

The Story of Ruth

Introduction

Naomi and her family moved to Moab, where her sons took Moabite wives. When the sons died and Naomi returned to Israel, the Moabitess Ruth came with her. Ruth became the great-grandmother of King David. What can we learn from this lovely woman?

Story

Long ago, in the time of the Judges, the Moabites were the most hated enemies of Israel. They had made war against the Israelites long and cruelly, and the things they had done were hard to forget. But when famine struck Israel, a wealthy man named Elimelech decided to overlook the long-standing quarrel with the Moabites. Concerned that there was no food for his family in Israel, he took his wife Naomi and their two sons to live in Moab, on a fertile plateau far on the other side of the Dead Sea.

For a time the family prospered. The Moabites respected Elimelech and made him an officer in their army. The two sons married Moabite women, Ruth and Orpah. But then Elimelech died, and after ten years his sons also died. Then Naomi and her daughters-in-law found themselves facing an uncertain future.

One day a caravan brought word that the famine in Israel had passed. To Naomi, this news was like the rainbow that appears after a storm. Feeling that she no longer had any reason to remain in Moab, Naomi made up her mind to return to her native land.

It was a sad farewell that Naomi bade her daughters-in-law. The three women stood at the dusty crossroads and the younger ones wept while old Naomi gently urged them to turn back.

"Go; each of you should return to her own mother's home. May God be as kind to you as you have been to me and my dead sons."

But Ruth and Orpah were both goodhearted women and did not like to see Naomi set out alone on the long and dangerous journey. Naomi argued with them. "Look at me," she said. "I am old. I have no more sons whom you may wed. But here in your own country, you may find husbands and perhaps have sons of your own."

Finally Orpah, the elder daughter-in-law, nodded her head in agreement. She kissed Naomi, and set off down the road back to her home.

Then Naomi said to Ruth, "Won't you follow

your sister's example? She has gone back, and so should you."

But Ruth, whose name in Hebrew means "friendship," answered Naomi with lovely words: "Entreat me not to leave thee, and to return from following after thee; for whither thou goest, I will go; and where thou lodgest, I will lodge; thy people shall be my people and thy God my God; where thou diest, will I die, and there will I be buried; the Lord do so to me, and more also, if aught but death part thee and me."

And Ruth traveled with Naomi into Israel, braving, as Naomi had done before her, the trials of a stranger in a strange land. And because Ruth was kind and good, Naomi's kinsman Boaz married her. The son of Ruth and Boaz was Obed; and Obed was the father of Jesse, and among the sons of Jesse was David, king of Israel.

Questions

1 What does Ruth's beautiful speech, "Entreat me not to leave thee," mean?

2 Is it easy to move to another neighborhood? To another country? Was Ruth brave to go back with Naomi?

3 What does this story tell us about strangers?

4 Does an enemy always remain an enemy?

The Field of Brotherly Love

7

Introduction

When King Solomon got ready to build the great Temple, he remembered that the sages had said it would be built "in a field of brotherly love." But first he had to find that field.

Story

The time had come to build a Temple to the Lord, but where to build it troubled the wisdom of even great King Solomon. The Lord, who had refused to let David build the Temple because his hands were covered with the blood of battle, promised David that his son Solomon might do so. But now King Solomon wondered where on earth such a Temple should be built. The sages had prophesied, "In a field of brotherly love." But where in the troubled world did one find such a field?

One night, restlessly turning on his ivory couch, the king heard a still, small voice in the gloom: "Awake, Solomon! Arise and go up to Mount Moriah in Jerusalem."

King Solomon awoke and left his couch. With

his long mantle flying around him, he strode out of the palace and walked toward Mount Moriah. He remembered, now, that a fertile field did stretch across Mount Moriah, but there was nothing special about the field that he could call to mind. The field had been left to two brothers. Each lived in a house built at opposite ends of the field. The first brother was married and the father of four children; the second brother lived alone. Together, they tilled and tended the field, and when the harvest was in, they divided the wheat equally between them.

When Solomon reached Mount Moriah, he saw only the brothers' two houses, pale in the moonlight. Except for the crickets chirping, the night was silent.

While the king waited in the silent field, the brothers were tossing on their beds, unable to sleep, worrying about each other. The first brother said to himself, "How fortunate I am! I

have a wife and children, and when I am old, my
children will care for me. But my brother has no
one. I must bring part of my wheat to him, so he
will have something to save for his future."

The second brother, in his house, thought to
himself, "Here I am, with only myself to feed.
But my poor brother has a wife and children to
care for. In all fairness, my brother should have
a larger share of the wheat than I. I shall bring
part of my wheat to him, secretly, in the night."

The two brothers got out of bed and each went
to the granary where he stored his crops. Stealing across the field in the light of the full moon,
their arms filled with sheaves of wheat, each was
too busy to see the other or to notice Solomon in
the distance. But the king saw them.

Each brother left his gift of wheat in the other's granary, then hurried back for more. But
when they reached their own granaries, they
were amazed to find that there was still as much
wheat as there had been in the beginning. Again
they carried sheaves across the field, and when
they returned home, again they found that they
had as much wheat as in the beginning.

All night they went back and forth, and when the sun rose, the two brothers met at last in the middle of the field. For a moment they only stared at each other. Then, as they began to realize what had happened and why their stores of wheat were not diminished, they threw their arms about each other and laughed aloud.

Then King Solomon knew why the still, small voice had sent him to this place. He had found the place he sought. And when King Solomon built the great Temple, he built it in the middle of the field on Mount Moriah, where two brothers, walking in opposite directions, had met in love and concern at dawn.

Questions

1 Where did the still, small voice guiding Solomon come from?

2 Why did the single man take wheat to his brother?

3 Why did the married man take wheat to his brother?

4 Why should a holy Temple be built on a field of brotherly love?

The Image

8

Introduction

Hillel explains to his class that a mitzvah *is a good deed. Then he goes off to the bathhouse—to do a mitzvah!*

Story

Once, when the great Hillel was teaching, a young man who was not one of his students wandered into his classroom. The lesson that day was about what it means to perform a *mitzvah*.

"A *mitzvah*," explained Hillel, "is a good deed. Whenever you do something to help men, or to honor God, you have done a *mitzvah*."

Hillel asked his students to name different kinds of *mitzvot*.

"Bringing friends back together after a fight," one of them said.

"Keeping the Sabbath," a second said.

"Making blessings over food," another volunteered.

The visitor thought these examples were very good, for they all gave honor to the goodness and glory of God.

Soon the lesson was over and the students left. As Hillel walked out of the classroom, the young man went up to him.

"Where are you going now, Hillel?" he asked.

Hillel pointed to a bathhouse that stood not far from the school.

"I am going to do a *mitzvah,*" he said.

"At the bathhouse?" exclaimed the young man. "What *mitzvah* will you do there?"

"Why, take a bath," replied Hillel.

"I do not understand," said the visitor. "How in the world can you do a *mitzvah* by taking a bath?"

"I will tell you," said Hillel. "Did you ever see the statues of the king which stand outside the great theater?"

The young man nodded, and Hillel continued speaking.

39

"Have you noticed how clean they are, how the workmen polish them over and over? Do you know why that is?"

"It is because those statues are made in the image of the king," answered the boy. "The king would be very angry if they were to become dirty. It would show a lack of respect."

"True," remarked Hillel. "Men work very hard keeping those statues sparkling to honor the king. In the same way, I feel my body must also be kept sparkling, for I am made in the image of God, the King of kings. So too, each of us is made in the image of the divine Creator, and to keep our bodies clean is to honor Him. That is why taking a bath is really doing a *mitzvah*."

Questions

1   Can you think of any *mitzvot* you have ever done?

2   In whose image were the statues made?

3   In whose image are we made?

4   Do you know where it says that we are made in the image of God?

5   Can you think of other things we might do to honor God in whose image we are made?

9 The King's Son

Introduction

A king offers his long-lost son anything in his kingdom, but the boy does not realize that he is a prince, and does not know how to make a suitable choice. Would you know what to ask for if you were given an opportunity to choose any gift you wanted?

Story

Rabbi Simha Bunam was a marvelous teller of tales. He had traveled far and wide. He had lived in large cities and in tiny hamlets. He knew men who had sinned and men who were pious and wise. One snowy evening, Rabbi Simha Bunam sat beside a glowing coal stove in a tiny cottage in a village in Poland, and told this story about the king's son:

Once there was a king's palace that was surrounded by four sets of walls. The outermost wall enclosed the town where the king's subjects lived. Within the town was a second wall that surrounded a magnificent garden planted with

41

every variety of flower and fruit tree. Inside the garden was a third wall protected by the king's army. And there was still a fourth wall which enclosed the king's palace with its many towers and turrets rising into the sky.

When the king's son, the little prince, was seven years old, a band of gypsy dancers came to the palace to entertain the king and his court. They wore gay clothes of red and green and blue, and they brought with them a dancing bear.

After the gypsies had gone, the king went to wish his son a good night, but the little prince was not to be found. At first the king thought that his son was somewhere in the palace, and he began to look through the many rooms. He went from one great hall to another, from one bedroom to another. He searched in the servants' quarters, and finally he looked in the towers and all along the parapets. But the little prince was gone!

Finally the king realized that the little prince must have gone away with the gypsies. He called out his army and ordered them to find the gypsies and bring back the prince. The army searched everywhere, but no one knew where they had gone. Some said they had gone to the forest, and some said toward the mountains. Some had seen them in the west, and some had seen them in the east.

Many years passed, and the little prince was brought up among the gypsies. He forgot the wonders of the palace. He forgot how he had played along the palace walls and seen the entire kingdom from the tall palace towers. He forgot his family, his playmates, the parades and carnivals, the fine clothes and festive parties.

The gypsies taught him to dance. They made him dance with a big bear whose fur was polished with grease. As they traveled from town to town, the past life of the little dancer faded away into memories of a dream, far away and long ago.

One day word spread through the land that the king was dying. He was calling for the missing prince. Anyone who could find the prince and return him to the palace would receive a huge reward. The gypsies wanted the reward, and they set out for the palace.

They passed through the gates of the first wall, and the dancing-boy looked about him at the town. He could not remember ever seeing so many people in one place before. So many smells, and so many sights, and so many sounds!

Then the gypsies passed through the gates of the second wall. When the dancing-boy saw the garden filled with beautiful flowers and ripe fruits, he thought he must have entered paradise. Then he passed through the gate of the third wall, and he saw the soldiers all marching together, like great mechanical dolls.

Then one of the gypsies talked with the guardian of the fourth wall, and soon they were inside the palace. The dancing-boy gazed with wonder at the walls of the palace, covered with glittering gold and polished brass.

"You are going to see the king," said the oldest gypsy to the dancing-boy. "He will give you great gifts. You may ask for gold, or silver, or rubies, or diamonds. And the king will reward us, too, for bringing you back to the palace."

When the dancing-boy was brought to the throne room, the king recognized him as his son. He paid the gypsies the reward he had promised, and sent them away.

Then the king said to his son, "The kingdom is yours. You may have anything that you desire. What do you wish for?"

The dancing-boy-prince looked down at himself and saw his bare feet and his torn shirt. He looked about him at the room draped in purple velvets and emerald satins, and at the silver

44

throne with its carvings. He did not remember the room. He looked at the king in his golden crown, and he did not remember his father.

Finally, the boy said, "I would like some warm clothing and a strong pair of shoes. How wonderful that would be."

When Rabbi Simha Bunam finished the story, he sighed and said, "We are all like the dancing-boy-prince. We always ask for little things, and forget that the whole world, full of God's glory, is ours. We always wish for the small needs of the hour, and forget that we are children of the King, our God."

Questions

1 Would you rather be the dancing-boy or the prince? Why?

2 Why do you think Rabbi Bunam gave a great sigh when he finished his story? What was he trying to say by telling this tale?

3 In order for us to be happy, do we need big things, or little things? Do we need both?

4 What little things are important? What big things are important?

45

The Peasant Who Pretended to Be a Rabbi

10

Introduction

The Dubner Maggid, a preacher and storyteller, drives from town to town, talking to the people. One day, his coachman wants to find out what it feels like to be famous. The Maggid and the coachman switch clothes and roles.

Story

In eighteenth-century Eastern Europe, preachers known as *maggidim* often traveled from town to town, delivering lectures and sermons and interpreting the Law. The Dubner Maggid was especially famed as a scholar whose piety did not keep him from understanding the problems and pleasures of the common people.

One day, while he was still on the road, his coachman called to him: "Rabbi, I've been a good driver, haven't I? Dubno, Vilna, Zamoscz. . . . There's not a place in the world I haven't driven you."

The Maggid smiled.

"So," said the coachman, "I would like to ask one favor. Wherever we go, the people pay you

great honor. Is it a crime to want to know how it feels to be famous? Though I am unable to read or write, if you were to exchange clothes with me for a day, the people would think that I was the preacher and you were the coachman. And they would honor me instead!"

Now the Dubner Maggid enjoyed a good joke as much as anyone, but he did not like to see his faithful driver make a fool of himself in front of the local scholars.

"And what if we do change places?" he asked. "What will you do when they ask you to explain some difficult passage in the Law? Why, you'll fall flat on your face!"

But the driver said, "Don't worry about that, Rabbi, I'll take my chances."

"Then here are my clothes."

So the two men undressed and traded clothes and the Maggid became a coachman and the coachman became a rabbi.

As they entered the town, all the people in it turned out to greet the famous "preacher." Leading the coachman into the synagogue, they shook his hand and said, "*Sholom aleichem,* Maggid," and bowed. The real rabbi followed at a humble distance, as a coachman should.

The "rabbi" was immensely pleased with his reception. Surrounded by the local scholars, he

47

sat in the seat of honor, quite satisfied with the way things were going, while the Dubner Maggid watched with twinkling eyes from a corner of the room.

Then someone spoke up. "Learned rabbi," he asked, "will you be kind enough to explain to us this passage in the Law? We have not been able to agree upon an interpretation."

"Oh, oh," thought the Maggid in his corner. "Now my friend has had it!"

With his brows pulled tight in concentration, the "rabbi" peered into the Torah placed in front of him, and the room was silent because no one wished to disturb him while he was thinking. Only the Maggid knew that the "rabbi" could not read one word of the Torah.

Suddenly the "rabbi" impatiently pushed the book away from him, rose and confronted the group around him, shouting: "Some scholars! Couldn't you ask me a question that would be worthy of my talents? Why, the passage you have pointed out to me is so simple that anyone could explain it. Even my coachman can explain it to you!"

With that, he called to the Dubner Maggid. "Driver, come here and explain the Law to these so-called scholars!"

Questions

1 Do you know what a parable is?

2 Do you think this story is a parable? Of what?

3 Do you think the coachman was a clever man?

4 Do you sometimes think someone is great because of the way he or she dresses?

5 Is that the right way to judge a person?

King David and the Frog

11

Introduction

King David is rightfully proud of his beautiful songs. But when he decides his songs are better than anybody else's, a good friend takes him down a peg or two. Now David had many friends. Why is this friend a gruff old bullfrog?

Story

King David had a harp which always hung on the wall above his bed. Often at midnight the wind came in the window and plucked the harp strings, playing a small song.

David always awakened when he heard the wind playing his harp. Then he would take down the harp and play it himself, while the wind sang along with him. David played a great many songs, and they were all songs which he had written himself. He sang his songs to God.

The songs which King David sang were very beautiful. Sometimes they were songs of joy, songs that said how glorious the world is and how good it is to be alive. Sometimes the songs offered thanks to God, and praised Him for His justice and goodness. Sometimes, in times of trouble, the songs begged God for help and understanding. But always they were beautiful, because they told of David's deepest and truest feelings.

One night David sang a wonderful new song, making it up at the very moment he was playing. When he had finished he quickly wrote the song down, so that he would not forget it. He was so pleased with his new creation and so proud of himself that he shouted into the night, "O Lord my God, there is no one in all Your wide world who sings such songs as I do!"

David's call echoed in the still night air. There was not another sound to be heard, except the low croaking of some frogs who lived in a pond not far from the palace. Then the sound of croaking became much louder, and suddenly a bull-frog jumped through the window and right into

David's room. The sound of his deep "Croak!" was now so strong that it filled the entire room.

David looked at the frog in amazement, but the frog was not the least bit afraid of the king. "King David," he croaked, "do not think that you are the only fine singer of songs. My family and I have been singing to God since long before you were born." And with that he jumped back out of the window, and disappeared as quickly as he had come.

For a while David sat perfectly still. He was much too surprised to know what to think. Finally he rose and carefully hung his harp back on the wall, and he smiled as he did so. For King David now realized what he had not known before: that God had planted a beautiful song in every creature in the world.

Questions

1 Do you know the name given to the songs David wrote?

2 Do you know the Hebrew word for these songs and what it means?

3 Name three kinds of songs David sang, according to the story.

4 What was the lesson the frog taught David—and us?

12

David and Goliath

Introduction

The young shepherd David, armed only with a slingshot, five smooth pebbles, and a mighty trust in God, goes out to do battle with the giant Goliath of the Philistine army. Who will win? Why?

Story

It happened in ancient times that the Philistines gathered their army to do battle against the Israelites. The two armies fought for many days, but neither one could triumph over the other; and the Israelites were very weary, and tired of battle.

Now in the land of Judah lived a young Israelite named David. His three older brothers were in the war, but David was too young to fight and remained at home to tend the sheep. One day his father sent him to the army camp with some supplies for his brothers. While David was talking with the soldiers a champion from the Philistine army, named Goliath, strode into the Israelite camp.

Goliath was a giant of a man. He wore an

enormous helmet, and clanking armor all of brass. It took two men to lift his gleaming shield. The spear he carried was like a small tree, and the ground shook when he walked.

"Ho there, Israelites!" roared Goliath with a mighty voice. "I offer you a challenge and a taunt. Choose a man from among yourselves to fight against me. If he can slay me, then the Philistines will surrender to the Israelites; but if I am the winner, then the Israelites must surrender, and become our slaves. Who has the courage to accept my dare?"

When they heard these words the Israelites trembled. "No man has a chance against the mighty Goliath!" they told each other. Only David the shepherd was not afraid of the gigantic warrior. "Who is this Philistine, that he should taunt the armies of the living God?" he demanded. "His challenge must not go unanswered."

So David went before Saul, the king, and said, "Be not afraid; I shall go and fight this Goliath." Saul looked down from his throne. He saw only a slender boy in shepherd's clothes. "You cannot fight against the Philistine," said Saul. "You are but a youth, while he is a powerful warrior who has known battle all his life."

Then said David, "I tend my father's sheep.

Once when a lion came and took a lamb from the flock, I went out after him, and struck at him, and rescued the lamb. Then when the lion reared up against me I caught him by his mane, and struck him again, and killed him. I did this also with a bear. Just as I slew the lion and the bear, I shall slay this Philistine, because he has taunted the living God. And the Lord who de-livered me from the lion and the bear will deliver me from Goliath."

When King Saul saw the faith and determina-tion of the young David, he said, "Go, and the Lord shall be with you." Then Saul dressed David in his own armor, a shining brass helmet and a great coat of mail, and he bound his own sword about David's waist. But David found Saul's armor heavy and strange. "I cannot take these; I am not used to them," he said. He took off the glistening armor and the sharp sword, and took instead his own wooden sling. He put the sling in his shepherd's bag along with five smooth stones chosen from a brook, and with these weapons he went to do battle against the mighty Goliath.

When the gigantic Philistine saw a small slender youth approaching him, armed only with a slingshot, he called to David scornfully, "I will squash you into powder, you who dare to chal-lenge me armed with a boy's playthings." But David replied, "You come to me with a sharp sword, a long spear, and a javelin; but I come to you in the name of the Lord of Israel, whom you have taunted. Today He will make me victor over you, so that all men may know that there is a God in Israel."

Then Goliath began to charge toward David, his sword held high. Quickly David drew a stone out of his bag and aimed his sling. The stone hit Goliath squarely in the forehead, and the giant fell to the earth with a mighty crash. David ran to where the slain Philistine lay. He took the dead man's sword, and with it cut off the head of the great Goliath.

When the terrified Philistines saw what had happened to their leader, they fled.

And so the Israelites triumphed over their enemies. When David returned from battle he was cheered in all the cities of Israel, with singing and dancing, with drums and stringed instruments.

And years later, David became king over all Israel.

Questions

1 "You come to me with a sword and spear, and I come to you in the name of the Lord" is a very beautiful quotation. What does it really mean?

2 Do you believe that right always wins over might?

3 Do you know personally any times that right won over might? How about the opposite—might winning over right?

The Burning Fields

13

Introduction

Even a great rabbi can make mistakes. In today's story, we read what happened when Simeon ben Yohai forgot that the world is filled with wonderful creatures and objects which serve God in various ways.

Story

Once there was a great rabbi named Simeon ben Yohai who had to live in a cave for many, many years. There he and his son Eleazar hid from the Romans, who had ordered the Jews to give up their Torah or be killed. Rabbi Simeon had chosen to continue to study the Torah in hiding.

What was it like to live in a cave? It was cold, especially at night, and it was dark and damp. The rabbi and his son could not see the sunshine, or feel the wind on their faces, or hear the song of the birds. All they had to drink was the water from a stream which flowed through the cave, and their only food was the fruit of a carob tree that grew right outside it.

But Rabbi Simeon and his son Eleazar were

content in their cave, for there they could pray
and study the Torah all the day long. There was
nothing to distract them—no other people, no
other tasks, no other joys. And so they spent
their hours reading the wisdom of the Torah,
the poetry of the Torah, and the wonderful stories of the Torah. Soon it seemed to them that
the whole world was in the dark cave, and that
all the light and beauty in it came from the holy
books.

Time went by. Day followed day and night
followed night. Summer came and winter went.
Years passed, year . . . after year . . . after year
. . . for twelve years.

Then one day a man came through the hills to the cave, shouting their names. "Rabbi Simeon," he called, "the Roman emperor is dead. The new emperor has changed the law. You are free now, free to return to Jerusalem and to your students!"

The rabbi and his son said a prayer of thanks to God and walked out of the cave into the sunshine.

Everything seemed strange. Their legs were so stiff they could barely walk. The light dazzled their eyes and the fresh wind felt harsh against their skin.

As they were making their way back to Jerusalem, stumbling and shielding their eyes from the sun, they came across a group of farmers tending their fields. The men chatted and sang as they cut the golden grain.

"How good it is, father, to see people again," exclaimed Eleazar. "How happy and alive they look!"

But Rabbi Simeon's face grew dark with anger and his heart began to ache. "I lived in a dark cave for twelve years," he cried, "hungry and cold, for the sake of the Sacred Books. These men move freely in the sunlight, but instead of studying God's law they pay attention to the land."

In his grief he cried out, "Hear, O Heavens!

May these fields that take men away from the Torah be destroyed!"

At this, there was a great crash of thunder and the heavens seemed to split apart. A bolt of lightning flashed down from the skies to the fields, and the grain burst into flame. The farmers fled, weeping in fear and in woe.

Soon all was silent. Before Rabbi Ben Yohai and his son lay the burned and blackened fields.

Then a voice was heard through the clouds of smoke rising from the ashes: "Simeon ben Yohai, have you come out of your cave to destroy My world? It is you who do not understand My Law. It is you who sin by forgetting why I gave the Torah to the world."

The words shook Rabbi Simeon like thunder out of heaven. Stunned, he turned to his son. "The Torah was given to us to study, was it not?" he asked him.

Eleazar's eyes turned to the charred remains

of the grain and the weeping farmers, and then back to his father. "I remember, before we fled to the cave, you told me why we study Torah. You said Torah teaches us how to live and to work, and to rejoice in each other and in God's world, every day of our lives."

The rabbi listened to his son's words, and then stood for many moments deep in thought.

Finally Eleazar touched his sleeve and said, "Father, let us go now. Let us return to the house of study."

Rabbi Simeon shook his head. "I am not yet ready to teach others," he said. "I still have much to learn."

And he went back into the cave for twelve months more.

Questions

1   Why did Simeon ben Yohai and his son hide in the cave?

2   Do you think it would be pleasant to live in a cave for twelve years?

3   Was Rabbi Simeon right to destroy the farmers' crops?

4   Should a man spend all his time studying? Should he never study? What else should a man spend his time doing?

14 The Window and the Mirror

Introduction

Isaac the miser decides to buy matzot *for the poor at Passover. What has happened to change his heart and his mind? He has learned to look beyond himself to the wide world outside his window.*

Story

Isaac was enjoying himself. He was adding sums on a piece of paper to see how much money he had made that week. There was a lot to count, for he was the richest man in the village.

There was a noise outside and he went to the window. Two children were climbing and jumping on his fence. He scowled.

"Go away, go away!" He tried to roar, but his voice came out a squeak. "Fences cost money!" The children stopped laughing. Slowly they backed away.

His gaze rested on the house across the way. It was a disgrace. The paint was peeling and the gate was broken. Right across from his fine big house!

A figure was hurrying down the road—Feivel the bookseller in his coat with the fur collar. The sight always annoyed him. Who was Feivel to put on airs? A nobody without two kopecks in his pocket. Of course, his coat was no match for Isaac's, which was all fur and reached to his boot-tops.

Isaac went back to his favorite pastime—counting his money. He heard a voice shouting, "Potatoes! New potatoes!" A peddler was calling his wares. Noise—noise—when Isaac was trying to count.

He returned to his figures. Soon he began to chuckle. It had been a good week, God be praised. A very good week.

A knock on the door; there stood the rabbi. It was an honor to have the rabbi call. A great honor. Isaac tried not to look annoyed at all the honor. He knew what the rabbi wanted—money for *ma'ot hittim,* the Passover fund for *matzot* for the poor. A good cause, yes—but there was no end to good causes. Why did they always come to Isaac? Because he worked hard and saved a little now and then? Well, he'd have to give something.

The rabbi was disappointed at the sum, but Isaac was firm. "It's all I can afford," he said. "I have expenses."

The rabbi's eyes seemed to look right through him. "Isaac," he said, "look out the window, and tell me what you see."

Isaac looked. "I don't see anything. Just the street. A few people."

The rabbi turned to a mirror on the wall. "Look in this mirror, Isaac." Isaac gazed into the mirror. "Now what do you see?" Even a rabbi can sometimes ask foolish questions, Isaac thought to himself.

"My face," he answered. "What else?"

"The window is glass, and the mirror is glass. The only difference between them is a little silver. Add that bit of silver, and you can't see through the glass any more. All you see is yourself." The rabbi's eyes were sad. "That's why you can't see anything through the window, Isaac. A little silver—and all you can see is yourself." With that, the rabbi was gone.

Isaac stood looking after him. He didn't feel like counting his money. He kept seeing the rabbi's eyes. And hearing his sad voice: "A little silver—and all you can see is yourself."

He went to the window. What was there to see? That shabby house over there? He stared at it. A woman was sweeping the walk—the widow who owned the house. Since her husband died, she had to take in boarders. She looked

65

small and frail. A thought struck him—the place was too much for her to take care of alone.

The children were standing in the street now, like two pale shadows. The boy was too thin; his legs were like sticks. The little girl—was she lame? Yes, she limped. He hadn't noticed before.

He saw something else. They needed food. And sunshine and fresh air. And a place to play.

Feivel was returning, bent under a heavy load, his coat hugged tight around him. Isaac stared hard. The coat was worn and thin, and the old scrap of fur wasn't much help against the wind. Poor old Feivel—he'd been wearing that coat as long as Isaac could remember.

"New potatoes! Come, housewives—buy my potatoes!" Yankel the peddler was hoarse now. It was getting dark and cold, but he was still out there, trying to take in a few more kopecks. Today was Thursday, and he wanted to buy fish and *halah* for *Shabbat*. Yankel had five children —or was it six? A man worked hard to feed six children. Yankel must be ready to drop.

Something was stirring in Isaac—something new and strange. He was seeing people for the first time. The silver wasn't getting in the way. How was that? Could it be the silver wasn't so important? Not as important as the widow, and the children, and the poor?

A thought came into his mind. Passover was coming, and the widow and her children didn't have money for *matzot*. A fine holiday they would have!

Suddenly Isaac put on his coat and started to run to the rabbi's house.

Questions

1   *Ma'ot hittim* means "wheat money"—money collected especially for Passover. Why did the rabbi have to go around and collect *ma'ot hittim*? How do we collect money for the needy today?

2   Sometimes it is very hard to make a living even when you try. Should the wealthier members of the community be responsible for the poor?

3   Is the silver in the mirror and the silver on the table the same? Explain why, or why not.

4   What was the difference between Isaac's concern for money at the beginning of the story, and at the end?

The King and the Drinking Glasses

Introduction

In this story, a wise rabbi uses everyday utensils, two drinking glasses, to teach a king how to rule. And we learn the best way to govern our relations with other people.

Story

A great dinner was being held to celebrate the reign of a new king in Judea. While everyone was eating and drinking, the king turned to a rabbi who was known for his wisdom.

"Rabbi," he said, "I wish to rule wisely, so that my people will live in peace and contentment. Can you advise me on how I can make my wish come true?"

The rabbi thought for a moment. Then he pointed to two drinking glasses on the table.

"Do you see these drinking glasses?" he said. "If I put hot drinks in them, they will crack. But if the drinks are too cold, they may well shatter too. However, if I temper the drinks so they are neither too hot nor too cold, the glasses will not break."

The young king shook his head. "I don't understand you, rabbi. You speak in riddles. What do drinking glasses have to do with my kingdom?"

The rabbi smiled. "I will tell you a story," he said.

And this is the story he told:

Before the Lord God made the earth, He tested His ideas on several trial worlds. In one of the first of His trial worlds, He decided that *Justice* would be king.

"Everyone will be given exactly the same treatment in my world," King Justice announced.

This king was true to his word. Each person who came before him, whether he was powerful and rich, or humble and poor, received exactly the same treatment, and all cases were decided according to the letter of the law.

In one of the first cases that came before King Justice, a poor shepherd was accused of losing four sheep from the flock he tended. His employer demanded payment for the lost sheep.

"Is it true that the sheep were lost while you were supposed to be watching them?" King Justice asked the shepherd.

"Please, your Majesty, try to understand," cried the shepherd. "I left my flock because I heard a cry for help. A traveler had fallen into

JUSTICE
will be
KING

69

the well where my sheep go to drink. I answered his cry; if I had not he might have drowned. I went back to my flock as soon as I could, but four sheep were missing."

"You deserve the gratitude of the man you saved," the king said. "But what you did for that man has nothing to do with this case. You must pay for the sheep."

And so the shepherd had to pay a whole month's wages for the sheep. As a result, his family starved.

Soon after, two women came before the court. One of them had a crooked finger. She pointed to the other woman and said:

"She pushed me and I fell and broke my finger. Now isn't it fair that the same thing should be done to her?"

"I didn't mean to hurt her," the other woman said. "We were at the market and there was such a crowd that I was pushed against her by someone else. I didn't hurt her on purpose."

"Nevertheless," the king said, "it was *you* who broke her finger. Therefore it is just that the same injury should be inflicted on you. An eye for an eye. That is justice."

And so the poor woman's finger was broken to pay for the injury she had accidentally brought to another.

MERCY will be QUEEN

Many cases were brought before King Justice and he handled each according to the letter of the law.

But God found that He was not satisfied with the result. There was too much *injustice* in the world. So God remade the world and placed a gentle lady named *Mercy* on the throne.

"In my world there will be forgiveness for everyone," said Queen Mercy.

True to her word, no one was ever made to pay for his mistakes or punished for any wrong he did. If a man stole an apple from another man's orchard, he was forgiven. If the owner of the orchard killed him for stealing, he was pardoned. Soon there was no rule of law at all. The people who were stronger took advantage of those who were weak.

Again, God was dissatisfied. "If I create the world and let mercy rule alone, sinners will multiply. But if justice alone governs, how will the world endure? Lo, I will use both justice and mercy, and I pray the world will survive."

When the rabbi finished his story, he said to the young king, "Now do you understand my riddle of the glasses?"

The king lifted the fragile glasses from the table.

"Yes," he said. "Just as I must temper the drinks I put into these glasses so they will not break, so I must temper *justice with mercy*."

The rabbi nodded. "You have understood. And may God be with you in your rule."

Questions

1   Would you want to live in a world of only justice? Why or why not?

2   Would you want to live in a world of only mercy? Why or why not?

3   Do you think the king was fair to the shepherd? To the old woman?

4   What did the glasses have to do with justice and mercy?

72

Rabbi Elijah and the Rich Man

Introduction

What is empathy? It is putting yourself in someone else's shoes. In this story, Mr. Poznansky is tricked into feeling empathy for the poor people of Lodz. It is a very clever trick that Rabbi Elijah pulls on Mr. Poznansky, because empathy leads to—can you guess? Sympathy.

Story

In the great town of Lodz there lived rich people and poor people. The rich people, of course, had plenty of good food to eat, wore elegant clothes, and lived in fine houses. The poor people had little to eat, not much to wear, and barely a roof over their heads.

In Lodz there also lived Rabbi Elijah, a good and clever man. He spent his time trying to persuade the rich people to give some of what they had to the poor people. That was not an easy task, but Rabbi Elijah was not easily discouraged. Every year he coaxed, pleaded, and argued, until one by one the wealthy citizens agreed to donate money to help the poor people.

One year the winter was especially harsh. Storm after storm brought whirling snow, wind, and bitter cold. The poor people of Lodz suffered terribly because they could not afford enough coal and wood to keep them warm. So Rabbi Elijah paid a visit to the richest man in the city. His name was Kalman Poznansky.

Kalman Poznansky hated to part with his money. He gave to charity only as much as duty required. Even then, Rabbi Elijah always had to do a great deal of talking before Mr. Poznansky was persuaded to donate some of his fortune to the poor. And so, on this day, when a servant came to Kalman Poznansky saying, "Rabbi Elijah is at the door, sir," the master of the house was far from pleased.

"What a bother!" he mumbled to himself. "Here he comes to tell me once again how much the poor are suffering and how little they have. Still, he is a respected man, so I suppose I had better go and meet him." He went to the door to greet Rabbi Elijah.

"Good day, Mr. Poznansky, I hope you are well," began the rabbi as soon as he saw the man

hold the door open. And immediately Rabbi Elijah began to talk, very fast, about a great number of things. He talked about politics, and about the new synagogue, and about the weather; he discussed the latest scandal and the latest marriage, and the price of milk and eggs. All this time Kalman Poznansky stood at the open door in his shirtsleeves. The icy wind gusted and whistled about him, and Mr. Poznansky shivered miserably. But the rabbi would not stop talking.

Finally Mr. Poznansky could stand it no longer. "I feel very cold, Rabbi," he said with chattering teeth. "Couldn't we discuss this inside?" Rabbi Elijah agreed, and followed his host indoors.

When the two men were comfortably settled in the well-heated study, Mr. Poznansky turned to his guest. "Rabbi, is it always your custom to hold conversations in unheated entranceways?"

Rabbi Elijah smiled. "Now I can tell you the purpose of my visit," he replied. "It is a hard winter indeed this year, and the poor are suffering terribly. I came to ask you for an especially generous charity gift."

"Yes, yes, but why did you keep me at the door so long?" Poznansky persisted. "Do you usually do so in such cold weather?"

"No, not usually," the rabbi responded. "But today I had a special reason. If we had come directly to this warm study, my talk about the sufferings of the poor would have meant little to you. But standing in that freezing wind for only a few minutes has given you some small idea of what it is like for the poor people to be cold all winter long. And therefore, Mr. Poznansky, I think your donation this year will be even larger than usual."

And indeed, so it was.

Questions

1 Did this story remind you of another story in this book? Which one?

2 Why is it so difficult for people who have money to share it with those who have not?

3 Would you give more *tzedakah* if you knew exactly to whom your money was going, rather than giving it to the United Jewish Appeal or the Jewish Federation Campaign? Why, or why not?

4 Are there other ways of giving *tzedakah* in addition to money? Can you think of examples?

17

From His Royal Highness, the Caliph of Arab Spain

Introduction

The Caliph writes a letter in which he questions how a Jewish poet made a friend of an enemy. Imagine that you have received his letter. What kind of answer could you give him?

Story

From His Royal Highness, the Caliph of Arab Spain, to his good friend, Omar, Royal Physician to the House of Arabia:

Greetings!

I write to tell you of a most strange thing which has happened here in my Royal Court and which I think will interest you. It is about our friend, the Jewish poet, Samuel ibn Nagdela.

You see, Omar, it all began at a festive dinner, when all the gentlemen and ladies of the palace were gathered together. A wonderful feast was served, and there was much laughter and joy.

Suddenly, a young man named Amir called out to all who could hear, "There is a man here

77

who does not belong to us. He is not a man of Allah, but he worships a different God. He should not be allowed here in the palace of the Caliph. His name is Samuel ibn Nagdela."

Now I am a great friend of Samuel, and I believe that the Jews and the Arabs are cousins and should live in peace. I was very surprised, and very angry.

"Enough!" I called out. "Amir, this is a very bad thing that you have done. Samuel is my friend, and no man should insult the friend of the Caliph. So I turn you over to Samuel. Samuel, you will torture Amir and cut out his tongue so that he may never say another evil word." Then the guards took Amir to Samuel's room.

The next day, as I was walking through the halls of the palace, I heard laughter coming from Samuel's room. Looking inside, I saw Samuel speaking and laughing with Amir.

"What is this?" I asked. "Is this not the man who insulted you, Samuel? Did you not cut out his evil tongue?"

Then Samuel said, "Amir is my friend now, your Majesty. I have taken away his evil tongue and replaced it with a kind one."

"But how have you done this, Samuel?" I asked. "How can a man replace an evil tongue with a kind one?"

"I have only been kind to him," Samuel answered.

But, Omar, I still do not understand how it was done, unless perhaps it was some kind of magic. Can you explain this thing?

Your Friend,
The Caliph of Spain

Questions

1   The Caliph said that since it was Amir's tongue that was evil, the tongue should be cut out. That is like "an eye for an eye." Is it a good idea to have justice of this sort?

2   What is prejudice? Who was prejudiced in the story?

3   What did the Caliph mean when he said that the Jews and the Arabs are cousins?

Jonah and the Gourd

18

Introduction

You know how Jonah went to sea and was swallowed by a great fish; he was trying to escape from the task God had given him, to convince the people of Nineveh to repent from their evil ways. Why did Jonah want to escape? And why was he unable to? This story tells what happened to Jonah after he got out of the belly of the fish.

Story

God called upon Jonah, the prophet, and told him to go to Nineveh and to tell the people there that God was greatly angered with them. But Jonah did not wish to go to Nineveh.

He thought, "What if I warn the people of Nineveh and say, 'Because of your evil ways your city will be destroyed'; and what if they repent and the Lord does not destroy their city? Then they will say that Jonah has told them tales and lies and is not a true man of God. Then they will drive me from their city and they will turn back to their evil ways."

So Jonah tried to run away from the Lord. But

in vain. For the Lord was everywhere. And everywhere He commanded Jonah to go to the city of Nineveh and warn them.

So Jonah journeyed three days' distance and came to the gates of Nineveh. And to each person who entered the city, Jonah said, "In forty days shall this city be destroyed, thus saith the Lord." And the words of Jonah, the prophet, were carried even to the King of Nineveh, and the king said, "Bring me this prophet."

Then Jonah was led into the city. Jonah listened to the bells of camel caravans resting beside the well, and he smelled the thousand smells coming from the market place, and it seemed good to him. But then Jonah saw people being beaten and robbed in the streets with none to help them. And so it was in the entire city—people arguing and fighting, hurting one another. And Jonah saw that it was evil.

When Jonah came to the king, he spoke his warning, "Thus saith the Lord, turn away from all evil or I shall destroy Nineveh even as I have made it great."

The king was sore afraid when he heard the word of the Lord, and he proclaimed the word in all the land. And all the people of Nineveh were frightened, and all fasted and prayed to the Lord to spare them. Jonah saw the praying and the fasting and he waited. But when the Lord saw the people were sorry, he had pity and did not destroy Nineveh.

Then Jonah was angry and he left the city and went up on a hill and sat beneath a tree. The sun grew hot and still hotter, until Jonah could barely stand it any longer. So the Lord caused a gourd to grow from a branch of the tree and it shaded Jonah's face from the sun. In the night, a worm came and ate the gourd. Once again the sun came and struck Jonah's forehead with its heat and now Jonah fainted.

As in a dream, Jonah heard the voice of the Lord, "Jonah, are you angry because of the gourd?"

Jonah said, "It is so, I am greatly angry."

And the Lord said, "You have pity on the gourd, though you did not grow it and though it was a small thing. And should I not have pity on Nineveh, that great city, wherein are many thousand persons, simple persons who do not understand the ways of God?"

Questions

1 Why did Jonah not want to go to Nineveh? What was he afraid of?

2 Are we afraid sometimes to tell the truth to someone? Why?

3 Do you think Jonah was a coward? Or was lazy? Why?

4 What is a gourd?

5 What was the lesson that God taught Jonah with the gourd?

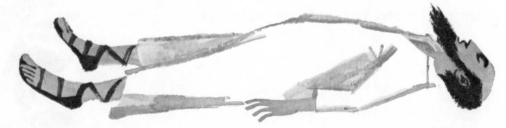

The Thief's Secret

19

Introduction

Chaim steals two plums from the king's orchard because he is poor and hungry. The king sentences him to be hanged. But Chaim knows this judgment is not just. How cleverly he tricks the king!

Story

There once was a very strict king who was known for his terrible temper. All the men of his court wore velvet slippers and approached him on tiptoe, for the slightest disturbance might cause the mighty king to fall into a rage.

One day a poor man named Chaim found his way into the royal orchard and stole two ripe plums. But before he could even take one bite, he was caught by the palace guards and brought before the king.

The king was very angry. "Stealing from my plum trees? My precious plum trees?" he roared. "Well, there has been too much stealing of late. You thieves must be taught a lesson. Chaim, you are sentenced to death for your crime."

The court gasped when they heard the king's order, but Chaim merely shrugged and said, "It is indeed a pity that I must lose my life for two plums, but it is a greater pity that my father's secret must now be lost as well."

When the king heard this he almost forgot his anger.

"Tell me your father's secret!" he commanded.

"There is a way to plant a pomegranate seed so that it will bear fruit the day after it is placed in the ground!"

"That is indeed remarkable," thought the king. "If I could learn this secret my fame would reach the far corners of the earth."

He turned to the prisoner and exclaimed, "Let us see you perform this deed, Thief!"

And so, while a page went to fetch a pomegranate seed, the king and all the men of his court went out to the garden and watched as Chaim dug a deep hole.

When the seed was brought Chaim lifted it carefully and said, "My lords, I need the help of one of you."

"How can we help you when we don't know the secret?" asked the king, frowning.

Chaim replied, "In order for this seed to bear fruit overnight, it must be planted by a man who has never taken anything that was not his. If the man has taken anything at all, the tree will not grow. Of course, I am a thief, so I cannot plant the seed."

On hearing this, the king turned to his noblemen and proclaimed, "My trusted prime minister will have the honor of planting this seed."

But the frightened minister replied, "Your Majesty, when I was just a young soldier, I took a silver sword that belonged to my friend."

The king turned from him angrily and held out the seed to his treasurer.

"But your Highness," stammered the treasurer, "I deal in sums every day. Perhaps once, in a moment of thoughtlessness, I subtracted too much."

The king offered the seed to each officer of state, but each had to refuse the honor. When the last nobleman had declined, the king shouted angrily, "Is there not one honest man in this court?"

Then Chaim spoke up quietly. "If I may be so bold, your Majesty, you are the only one among us who is able to plant the seed."

And now, when the honor was offered to him, the king remembered that he had once kept a ring that belonged to his father. The seed dropped from his hand.

When Chaim saw that the king himself could

not accept the seed he cried out, "You are all mighty and powerful and want for nothing and yet you cannot plant the seed; while I who stole two plums to ease my hunger am to be hanged."

Everyone stood in silence and looked at the king. At last the king turned to Chaim and said, "You are a clever man, for you have shown that none of us is perfect. You are hereby pardoned for your own misdeed."

Chaim bowed and ran off through the garden. As the king watched him leave, he vowed to remember his own deeds and to judge all men with greater compassion.

Questions

1 We spoke about parables before. Is this story also a parable? About what?

2 Which commandment says "Thou shalt not steal"?

3 Was the sentence by the king equal to the crime? Why or why not?

4 Was Chaim stupid or clever? Why?

The Wind and I

20

Introduction

When the wind ruled Talpiyot, he wanted no neighbors. But one man cared so much for that land that he resisted the wind's worst blows. In the end, both wind and man moved side by side through the shade of the Talpiyot trees. Let's see how they made peace with one another in a land so fiercely fought over.

Story

Many years ago the wind ruled the land called Talpiyot, which is near the city of Jerusalem. He swept the mountain, the valley, and the open plain, as if the land belonged to him alone.

I happened once to be in Talpiyot and I saw that it was a beautiful place. I was walking all alone when the wind came across me.

"What are *you* doing here?" he asked.

"Me?" I said. "I'm taking a walk."

He slapped me on the head and tossed my hat down. I bent over to pick it up. He turned my coat upside down over my head. While I was trying to straighten it out he threw me to the ground, roaring with laughter. When I stood up he beat against me and shrieked, "Get out of here!"

I saw that I could not argue with the wind, so I went away.

I tried to live in the city, but soon my feet brought me back to Talpiyot. I remembered what the wind had done to me, so I pitched a tent to protect myself.

One night, as I was sitting in my tent, the candle went out. I left the tent to see who had put out my light and I found the wind outside.

"What do you want?" I asked him.

He squeezed my mouth and he slapped my ears. I turned and ran back to my tent. He pulled up the tent-pegs, tore away the rope, overturned the tent and threw it away.

I returned to the city, and there I dreamed of fresh air. And since there is no air as fresh as the air of Talpiyot, I returned there. But this time I took wood with me, to build a cabin.

I shall never forget my cabin. It was small, but

there was room enough for a man like me who does not look for big things.

One day as I sat in my cabin the wind came along and asked, "What is this?"

"This is a cabin," I said.

He laughed. "I have never seen anything so funny as this thing that you call a cabin."

I also laughed. "So, now you have seen something that you never saw before."

He laughed again and told me, "I will inspect it."

The wind inspected the door. The door splintered and fell. He inspected the windows. The windows shattered. Finally he went up to the roof. It groaned and collapsed to the ground.

The wind laughed once again. "Now where is the cabin that you built?"

I also asked, "Where is my cabin?" But I did not laugh.

I went back to the city once more. There I decided to build a house in Talpiyot truly strong enough to resist the wind. I bought heavy timber, large stones and mortar. I hired workers to lay a good foundation and build the house solidly.

When the house was finished, the wind came to pay me a visit. He howled around the walls and over the roof, but could find no way to get in. Finally he banged on the window.

"Who is knocking at my window?" I asked.

He chuckled. "A neighbor."

"What does a neighbor want on such a stormy night?"

He laughed. "I've come to give my neighbor a housewarming."

"And does a neighbor usually come in through the window like a thief?" I asked.

He knocked on the door.

"Who is knocking at my door?" I asked.

The wind said, "It is I, your neighbor."

"Come in, neighbor," I said.

"But the door is locked," the wind howled. "Open up!"

"I'm afraid of the cold," I said. "When the sun comes out, I'll open the door for you."

When the sun came out I opened the door, but the wind was not there. I stood in front of my house and breathed the still air. Then I saw that there were no trees or flowers. There was nothing outside my house but dirt and rocks. I decided to plant a garden.

I worked very hard to get the ground ready. Then I planted some young trees. Rain came and watered them, dew came and made them blossom, the sun came and made them grow. Before very long I had many trees thick with branches.

I made a bench and I sat in their shade.

One night the wind returned and struck at the trees, but the trees stood firm. They struck back at the wind. When the wind beat at the trees again, they struck back a second time. Finally the wind was out of breath. He turned and went away.

Today, since the wind has been beaten down a bit, he acts like a gentleman. And since he treats me like a gentleman, I treat him in the same way. When he comes for a visit, I ask him to rest with me on the bench in the garden, among the trees. He comes and sits there, bringing the freshness of the mountain air with him. We never talk about the way he used to act. And when he leaves I ask him to come again, like a good neighbor. For actually I like him very much. Perhaps he even likes me.

Questions

1 The storyteller lived in Talpiyot. Do you think he loved the place in which he lived? Why do you think so?

2 A symbol is something that represents something else. The wind and the storyteller are each symbols. What is the writer a symbol of? What is the wind a symbol of?

3 Who do you think won the battle over the land of Talpiyot?

 **21**

How the Helmites
Bought a Barrel of Justice

Introduction

*The rich grow richer and the poor grow poorer;
but the wise men of Helm decide this is unjust.
And if there isn't any justice in Helm, what is
the wise thing to do? Why, buy some and bring it
home, of course!*

Story

In the days before business came to Helm, the
people were neither rich nor poor. Everyone was
content. But now, after the Helmites went into
business, the poor came to be jealous of the rich
and the rich came to fear the poor.

The rich ate the finest foods and wore expensive garments, while the poor suffered. Even in
the synagogue, the well-to-do would be seated in
their own pews at the East Wall near the Holy
Ark, while the poor would stand squeezed together behind the pulpit.

Finally, one summer Sabbath the long-suffering poor stopped the services and appealed to the
rabbi:

"Rabbi, why do the rich live on milk-and-honey, while we live on air?" cried a cobbler lad.

And before the rabbi could answer, came another cry from a tailor's apprentice:

"Why do the rich wear silks and stuff themselves with choice meats, while we go around in cotton rags and begrudge ourselves even a little soup cooked from bones?"

Then came a thunderous shout from the midst of the crowd, "O Rabbi, there is no justice in Helm!"

The rabbi took a pinch of snuff, sneezed twice, then answered slowly:

"True, there is no justice in Helm. But it must be somewhere, since the Holy Torah guarantees it. Therefore let us send two messengers out into the world to buy some justice and bring it back to Helm—enough for rich and poor alike."

And so the two messengers set out to buy some justice. But wherever they asked for justice, they were given the same reply:

"No use looking. If we knew where to get some, we'd sell the shirt off our back to buy it."

The Helmites rode on until they came to Warsaw. There, two rogues caught sight of them wandering through the streets. Being on the lookout for some easy money, the rascals went up to the Helmites and said:

"Friends, how would you like to get a good bargain? We can sell you the Vistula Bridge cheap, or if you can't use the bridge, we can sell you the Warsaw Synagogue."

Replied the Helmites: "No, good folks, we don't want to buy the bridge. And why would we need the Warsaw Synagogue when we have a synagogue of our own in Helm?"

"And what is it that two such wise men from Helm seek in Warsaw?" politely asked the rogues.

"Justice is what we seek," responded the Helmites. "We have traveled far and wide and cannot find a crumb of justice to save our lives."

Replied the rascals: "Look no further, Helmites. We'll sell you as much justice as you want."

The messengers from Helm asked eagerly: "Can you sell us a whole barrelful?"

"Well," said the swindlers, "justice is an expensive article. But if you can afford it, we'll manage to get you a barrelful."

A few hours later, the knaves delivered a barrel of justice to the messengers, who handed over two thousand gold pieces. At last their quest was ended!

There was great rejoicing in Helm. The messengers had returned. After elaborate ceremonies in the town square, Mottel the Mayor had the honor of opening the precious barrel. He pried open the cover while all of Helm crowded around.

As the cover was lifted, the foul odor of rotten fish assailed their nostrils. Springing back in horror, Mottel cried:

"Alas, the justice is spoiled!"

And now a wailing arose as the Helmites repeated to one another: "Alas, the justice is spoiled! What shall we do?"

Whereupon Gimpel, the richest man in Helm, exclaimed: "Take heed, O ye Helmites who complain of the justice of Helm." And pointing to the barrel, he bellowed: "That's the kind of justice you have in the rest of the world!"

The young cobbler lad sprang up to answer Gimpel: "Poor people of Helm, listen to me. If there is no justice in Helm, and if the justice of the world has been spoiled, then it doesn't matter what we do. We can do whatever we want."

The tailor's apprentice took up the cry: "The rich are few, we are many. No one can stop us."

"Let's break into the shops," shouted the cobbler lad, "and take whatever we need."

"Aye, aye!" clamored the poor people of Helm.

The rich became alarmed. They called a Town Meeting, and invited everyone to attend. There was thinking and talking for seven days and seven nights, and at last they came to a brilliant compromise:

"From this day on whenever an ox is slaughtered, let the entire animal consist only of the choicest parts. Then there will be no difference which part one buys.

"Likewise, let it be known to all that the entire synagogue is the East Wall and center pews. Then there will be no difference where a person sits.

"Likewise, let there be no distinction between satin and gingham, silk and cotton. Let all materials be alike. Then it will make no difference what sort of clothes one wears.

"But if the rich are foolish enough to wish to pay more in order to sit at the *former* East Wall; likewise, if they desire to pay more for the *former* choice meats, and for the *former* silks and velvets —then let them be welcome to their foolishness."

And so it was done. All was peaceful again in Helm. Both the rich and poor were content. For the rich, everything was as of old. Yet for the poor, times had changed. They went about, saying:

"Gone are the old, unhappy days when the rich lived on milk-and-honey and we lived on air. Now, all are equal!"

Questions

1   Have you ever heard any other Helm stories? Are they funny only, or is there a point to them?

2   Does this one have a point? What is it?

3   Was the Helmites' approach to capturing justice silly? Was their conclusion silly too?

4   What is justice?

5   Do you know someone to whom an injustice was done? Tell about it.

22

The Education of Alexander

Introduction

Alexander the Great ruled all of the known world, but when he tried to enter the Garden of Eden, an angel turned him away. Why? And why did the angel give him such a strange present?

Story

Young Alexander of Macedonia had studied the writings of the Greek philosophers and scientists with the wisest men in the world, and was a very clever young man. He was also handsome and brave, and by the time he was thirty he had become a powerful king, the conqueror of all the known world. He traveled everywhere, inspecting all parts of his empire. At last his travels took him to the Land of Israel.

One day he stopped at a well to eat his lunch. It was fish that had been salted so that it would not spoil. As one of his servants rinsed away the salt with water from the well, the fish suddenly gave off an aroma sweeter than perfume. "This well must lead to the Garden of Eden," Alexander cried, "for its waters smell sweeter than any other water in the world."

99

Now the Garden of Eden was the one place that Alexander had never seen or conquered. "I will trace the well to its source," he said, "and learn what I may find."

Following the gentle stream until he came to the gate of the Garden of Eden, he knocked loudly, shouting, "Open this gate for me!"

"And who are you?" a voice answered.

"I am Alexander the Macedonian, conqueror of the world!"

"And who is Alexander, that he may enter? This is the abode of the blessed, the just and the peaceful. Though you rule nations, Alexander, you do not rule yourself rightly, and therefore you have no admittance here. Go back; conquer your inner world."

As much as Alexander stormed and railed, he could not enter the Garden of Eden. "At least," he pleaded, "give me some proof to show that I have reached the gates of this Garden; I am a king, and receive gifts of tribute wherever I travel."

So the guardian of the gates handed him a small gift, saying, "Take this and weigh it against all the gold you have received in tribute."

Horrified, Alexander discovered that he held in his hand a man's eye. But he called for a pair of scales. He placed the eye on one scale and

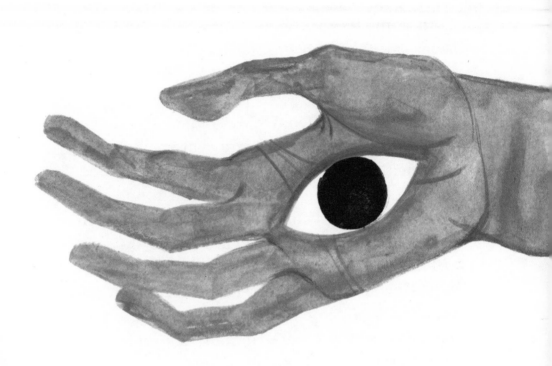

tried to balance the other with a piece of gold. To his astonishment, he found that the eye outweighed the gold. He added another gold coin, and then another. But no matter how huge the quantity of gold he heaped on the left, the pan on the right side of the scales sank ever more heavily. "Is there nothing greater than this useless eye?" he wondered.

Some rabbis happened to be passing by just then, and Alexander prevailed on them to explain this strange phenomenon.

"It is the eye of a man," they said, "which is never satisfied with the treasure it sees."

But Alexander persisted: "How am I to believe you?"

"Thus it is written, O Alexander," the rabbis answered: "Death and the grave are never satisfied; neither are the eyes of man." The rabbis then scooped some dust from the ground and covered the eye completely. At once the pan containing the eye shot upward to the sky.

Then Alexander walked away slowly, thinking: However I have stretched and bent the boundaries of the earth, my end will be under the earth; surely I leave nothing behind me except that which I give to others.

Questions

1 Who was Alexander, and why was he called "the Great"?

2 Did the guardian of the gate in the Garden of Eden consider Alexander to be "great"? Why?

3 Why did the eye outweigh the gold?

4 How did the rabbis prove their answer? What did the dust symbolize?

5 What did Alexander finally come to realize?

23 Rabbi Joshua and the Messiah

Introduction

Each of us has a great many tasks. As we grow older, we take on even more tasks and responsibilities. Why? What difference does it make whether we fulfill our responsibilities or not?

Story

Every day, for as long as he could remember, Rabbi Joshua ben Levi prayed for the coming of the Messiah. But the Messiah did not come, and Rabbi Joshua was beginning to give up hope.

"Why have my prayers gone unanswered?" he asked himself. "Is there something wrong with the way I am praying?"

Rabbi Joshua was so troubled that he could not sleep. He rose from his bed, left his house, and went walking through the night. He passed through the streets of the city, through the gates, and out into the silent countryside. He stopped and looked about him—at the deep black sky sprinkled with stars, at the trees whose leaves were silver-edged by the moonlight, at the tiny wildflowers whose petals were curled tight against the night chill.

Rabbi Joshua sat down to rest. He had not been sitting long when the Prophet Elijah appeared before him. It was not the first time Elijah had come to Rabbi Joshua, who thought of the Prophet as his friend.

"Elijah," Rabbi Joshua said, "there is a question I would like to ask you. Every day I pray for the coming of the Messiah, but my prayer is never answered. Can you tell me when the Messiah will come?"

Elijah smiled. "Go and ask him."

"Please don't joke with me," said the Rabbi. "You know I can't ask the Messiah if he isn't here."

"I'm not joking," Elijah said. "Go and look for him at the city gate. That's where he is."

Rabbi Joshua sighed. "The city gate is always so crowded with people, I don't think I could find my own brother there. Besides, how would I know him?"

"Look among the people who are poor and

sick," Elijah answered. "He is one of them, and he is covered with sores like all the others. The only thing different about the Messiah is the way he removes his bandages. While the others take off all of their bandages at once and then put them back, he takes off only one bandage at a time and puts it back before he takes off another. He does this so that he will always be ready to go if someone needs him."

Rabbi Joshua was very excited and hurried back to the city. In the morning he went to the gate and looked among the poor and sick. Just as Elijah had said, there was one man, and one only, who changed his bandages one at a time.

"Messiah," said Rabbi Joshua to the man.

The man quickly retied the bandage he was taking off and stood up. "I am here," he said.

"Our people need you," the rabbi said. "When will you let them know that you have come?"

"Today," the Messiah answered.

"But the day is half gone, and they still do not know about you."

"I am ready to let them know today," said the Messiah.

Rabbi Joshua hurried home and waited for news that the Messiah had come. But evening came and nothing happened.

That night again Rabbi Joshua could not

sleep. He rose from his bed and went out into the countryside. This time he called for Elijah, and when the Prophet appeared, Rabbi Joshua said, "The man you said was the Messiah lied to me. He told me he would come today, and now the day is gone, and he is not here."

"He did not lie," Elijah said. "He is speaking to you with the truth of the Bible, for it says 'Today shall I come, if only all of you would listen to my voice.'"

Elijah disappeared, and Rabbi Joshua started back again to the city. He did not know what to think. He wondered at the meaning of Elijah's words. The night was so silent that even the sound of a moving leaf could be heard. Suddenly he heard someone singing. The voice was so clear and sweet that Rabbi Joshua followed it around the side of a hill. There in the starlight he saw a young shepherd, singing to his sheep.

"Shepherd," said Rabbi Joshua, "why do you waste your voice on a flock of sheep? You should come to the city. When the people find that your voice is so beautiful they will gather together to listen to you."

The shepherd said, "Shall I wait to sing until the people are ready to listen? Many pass this way each day while I am singing, and they do not hear me. But I will not stop singing, just as the sun will not stop shining when there is no one around to see its light or feel its warmth. The world would be worse if it were not so, for who knows when someone like you may come by and be ready to hear me."

Rabbi Joshua smiled. "Shepherd," he said, "you are not only a good singer, you are a teacher. For you have taught an old rabbi a lesson."

And the meaning of Elijah's words became clear to him:

The Messiah is always there for those who are ready to receive him.

Questions

1   What is a Messiah?

2   Do you know any of the things that are supposed to happen when the Messiah comes?

3   What does the Messiah mean when he says, "I shall come today if all of you will listen to me."

4   Do you think the time will ever come when *everybody* will want to listen to the Messiah? Can we help that time to come?

The Old Man and the Serpent

Introduction

The Torah says that man and the serpent shall always be enemies. In this story, an old man takes pity on the serpent and finds his kindness repaid with evil. His life is saved by a wise man who shows him that his first responsibility is to obey God's commandments.

Story

One very cold day an old man left the warmth of his fire to walk through his fields. He carried a stick to help him over the rough ground and also to protect him. As he walked, the old man found a snake lying very still on the ground. He raised his stick to kill the snake, but it did not move. The man saw that the snake was frozen from the cold and was not able to move.

The old man felt pity for the snake, so he held it close to his body to warm it. Soon the snake began to get stronger, but still it made believe it was very weak. All at once, when it was very strong again, the snake wound itself around the old man and began to crush him.

The old man cried out in fear, "Why do you want to kill me? Haven't I just saved your life?"

The snake laughed as he spoke to the old man. "The Holy Torah says that the snake shall bruise the heel of man," said the snake.

The old man was very frightened. He asked the snake to go with him to a court of law to have the case judged.

"Who will be the judge?" asked the snake.

"Let us walk along the road," said the old man, "and whomever we meet shall be our judge."

The snake, very sure of winning his case, agreed to go along. So the old man started off down the road with the snake still wound tightly around him.

On the road, the old man and the snake met a big, strong ox, who was resting after working hard all day. The old man ran up to the ox.

"Tell the snake that it is wrong for him to kill me," said the old man. "I have just saved his life!"

"It says in the Torah that the snake and man are enemies," said the snake. "Therefore, I must be right to crush him to death."

The ox agreed with the snake. "You did a kind deed," said the ox to the old man, "but the snake must return it with an evil deed. In this world we always return good with evil."

They started off again and the snake tightened his hold on the old man. They walked on until they met a donkey who was drinking from a cool spring on the side of the road. Both the snake and the old man told the donkey the same stories they had told to the ox.

"Of course the snake is right," agreed the donkey. "To return good with evil is the way of nature and the world."

The old man did not feel that he was being judged fairly. He asked the snake to go with him to Jerusalem to find a judge. The snake, still not worried, agreed.

On the way, the old man and the snake stopped to watch a noble young man standing near a large hole in the ground. The young man had lost his beautiful walking stick in the pit. He told his servants to fill the pit with water, and when they had done so the stick floated to the top, so that the young man could reach it easily.

The old man saw that the young man was very wise, and decided to ask him for help.

The young man agreed to judge the case. He listened to the old man tell how he had saved the

life of the snake. He also listened to the snake tell how it was his duty to kill the old man. After hearing both stories, he spoke.

"First," he told the snake, "you must loosen your hold on the old man, for it says in the Torah that when two men are judged, neither shall have the advantage."

"Now," he asked the snake, "why do you want to kill the old man?"

"It says in the Torah," said the snake, "'You shall bruise the heel of man.'"

"It also says in the Torah," said the young judge, turning to the old man, "'You shall bruise the head of the serpent.'"

The old man raised his stick. He hit the serpent over the head and killed it.

Later the old man learned that the wise judge had been Solomon, the son of King David.

Questions

1 Is it natural for the snake and the man to be enemies?

2 Were the ox and the donkey right when they said good is returned with evil?

3 How do you know that the young man near the hole was wise?

4 What is this story trying to tell us?

The Puzzle of "Just Enough Men"

Introduction

The Midianites would attack Israel, seize its harvests, and burn the villages and farms, but young Gideon refused to be frightened. Instead, he rounded up an army and saved the day for the Jews. But why did he select his army in such a strange way? And why did he want a small army rather than a large one?

Story

Long ago, when the children of Israel lived in their own land and were farmers, a people called the Midianites were their enemies. The Midianites would wait until harvest time, and then they would come with great armies to take the crops away from the Israelites and burn their fields.

But there lived in Israel a young man whose name was Gideon, the son of Joash. Gideon was heartsick when he saw the Midianites come to get the grain which he had sown and tended with such hard labor.

One night, he went to the place where the Midianites worshiped their god, Baal. He smashed the idol and broke the altar. And in the morning, Gideon sent twelve messengers to the tribes of Israel, to tell them what he had done.

Now when the people heard what Gideon had done, they said, "Here is a man who will lead us against the Midianites who oppress us." And they came to join him. When Gideon counted the number of men who had come, he saw that there were more Israelites with him than there were Midianites.

So Gideon said to his servant, Purah, "Look, here are enough men to defeat all the armies of the Midianites."

But Purah shook his head. "These men can not win the battle, Master," he said.

"What do you mean?" asked Gideon.

So Purah took Gideon to one of the many large campfires and whispered to Gideon, "Listen to what the men say to one another."

One man said, "The tribe of Reuven is the strongest tribe. You will see how we defeat the Midianites. We are the greatest tribe of Israel."

"Not so!" said another man. "The tribe of Judah is best. We are braver and stronger than Reuven's tribe."

"Never," said a third man. "The tribe of Benjamin will be the champions of Israel."

"You see, Master," said Purah, "they are not

interested in defeating the Midianites. They only wish to see which is the strongest tribe. An army cannot win unless all the men in it work together."

Then Gideon said sadly, "You are right."

All night Gideon sat beside the fire and prayed for guidance in what he should do. When morning came, Gideon gathered all the men together. "There are too many people here," Gideon said. "Whoever is afraid, let him go home now."

Then many men returned to their homes. But still there remained ten thousand men.

So Gideon said to Purah, "See, now we are fewer in number than the Midianites. Can we win?"

And Purah answered, "No. For the army of the Midianites fights as one man, but our army still argues and boasts."

And Gideon listened again, and saw that it was true.

Then Gideon prayed to God again, and God spoke to him and told him what to do.

Gideon brought the men to the fountain of Ein Harod and told them all to drink. He said to Purah, "If a man drinks while kneeling, let him be sent home. But if he scoops up the water into his hands and drinks it as a dog drinks from his bowl, then he shall stay with me."

All the men drank. Most of them drank while kneeling, and were sent home. But each man who drank from the palm of his hand, as a dog drinks from his bowl, stayed with Gideon.

Now there were only three hundred men in Gideon's army, and he was greatly afraid. But Purah was calm. "Look," he said. "The men talk together as friends. They are united. This small group will defeat all the Midianites, because they will work together."

Then Gideon said, "You are very wise, Purah, very wise."

In the night Gideon woke his men quietly and said to them, "Arise now, for the Lord will give Midian into our hands. We will surprise them as they sleep." And Gideon devised a very clever plan of surprise attack, and the army of Midian was defeated.

Then peace returned to the farmers of Israel.

Questions

1 Are the children of Israel farmers today?

2 Is it right for anyone to take away what another plants and tends?

3 Can you guess one of the reasons why the men who kneeled to drink were sent home?

Yossel and the Tree

Introduction

Yossel talked all the time. He was so busy talking that he forgot to think. Luckily for him, he received two gifts from a tree! First it gave him lunch. And then what did it give him?

Story

There was once a man named Yossel who loved to talk. He loved the sound his voice made, and he loved always to be saying something, no matter whether it was wise or foolish. Yossel liked talking so much that he practiced speaking in many voices: a low rumbling drone, a high fast chatter, a slow soothing singsong. He practiced rolling his *r*'s and being very clear about his *t*'s and *ing*'s. He even practiced phrases that he could use at the proper time, like "It must be admitted," and "to be sure," and "beyond the slightest doubt." Sometimes they didn't make sense.

Yossel was very proud of his skill in speaking, but when the townspeople saw him coming, they would whisper, "Here comes Yossel the chatterbox," and hurry on their way so that they would not have to listen all morning to another silly speech.

Yossel talked a great deal, but he rarely worked. So he had plenty of spare time. One fine day he went walking in the countryside. As he walked he talked, carefully pronouncing any fancy phrase that popped into his head.

"How beautifully I speak!" he said to himself. "What a talented man I am!"

It did not take long before Yossel grew hungry. But since he was not as wise as he was talkative, he had not thought to bring any food with him. "Oh dear. I certainly would like something to eat," he thought. Then he noticed a tree whose branches were laden with ripe fruit. Hungrily he picked some of the fruit and tasted it. Delicious! Soon he had made a fine meal of the fruit and was sitting happily under the tree, his belly full, practicing yet another new speaking voice.

Yossel looked up at the branches above him. Suddenly he sat up and spoke to the tree. "Why don't you trees talk?" he demanded. "No one has ever heard your voice!"

Then the tree replied, "We don't have to talk about ourselves, or even to talk at all. We offer sweet fruit, not mere words. Our fruits speak for us."

Questions

1 What adjectives would you use to describe Yossel?

2 Do you know people like Yossel who love the sound of their voices?

3 Have you ever heard the expression "actions speak louder than words"? What does it mean?

Introduction

An old man named Jacob received from the king a basket of gold in return for a basket of figs. Why won't the king make the same trade with somebody else?

Story

Early one morning an old man named Jacob was out digging holes in the ground. He had not been digging long when he was approached by a group of men on horseback—not just ordinary men, but the king and his royal guards, out for a morning ride. The king was amazed to see such an old man working so hard. He reined his horse to a sudden stop and immediately began asking questions.

"How old are you, old man?" he shouted down from his horse.

"I am one hundred years old, your Majesty," Jacob replied.

"Why does such an old man as you work so hard?" the king continued. "And what is the purpose of those holes you are digging?"

"I am digging these holes because I am going to plant fig trees," Jacob explained.

"Fig trees! Hmmm," said the king. "As it happens, I am very fond of figs myself. In fact, I would rather eat figs than anything else. But surely it will take years before figs grow on your trees, and you are a very old man."

"Yes, your Majesty, you are quite right," replied Jacob. "I may not live to see the fruit on the trees, but that does not concern me. Many times I have eaten figs from trees that were planted before I was born. If I do not live to eat figs from these trees, then my children, and their children, and others too, will eat them."

The king was impressed by Jacob's answer. "You are a good and generous old man," he told Jacob. "I hope that God grants you many more years, so that you are able to taste the sweet fruit of your trees. If that should happen, bring some of the figs to me." Then the king and his royal guards galloped away.

The old man lived for many more years. His trees grew tall and leafy, and one day they brought forth fruit. Jacob filled a basket with the figs and went to see the king.

The king did not recognize Jacob when he was shown into the royal audience hall. The king only knew that this was the oldest man he had ever seen. Then Jacob approached the throne with the basket, saying, "Your Majesty, I have brought you some figs from the trees I was planting one morning when you were out riding." Suddenly the king remembered the old man who had been working hard so many years ago. He tasted a fig from the basket. "In all my life I have never eaten so sweet a fig," he declared. And after thanking Jacob most sincerely, he instructed his servants to empty the basket carefully and to fill it with gold coins. "It is a fair exchange," insisted the king. "I am extremely fond of figs."

Jacob thanked the king and returned home. Soon the whole town was buzzing with the news that the king had given the old man a basket of gold in return for a basket of figs. A certain greedy woman immediately began to nag her husband about this.

"Instead of just sitting about the house you could be out making our fortune," she complained. "If you were not such a dolt you would know what to do without my telling you. Now go pick a basketful of figs and take it to the king, and bring it home filled with gold!"

The woman's foolish husband did not quite understand how such an exchange would be made, but he thought there was no harm in trying, so he did as she instructed. When he was brought before the king, he offered his basket, saying, "I have here a basket of figs which I would be happy to give you in exchange for a basket of gold like that you gave to the old man."

When the king heard these words he grew red with rage. "I gave the old man a gift whose worth was equal to the gift he gave me," he said. "Now I shall repay you as your gift deserves." He leaned over and in a low voice told his guard exactly what he wanted done.

The guard approached the villager. "Come with me," he said. "I will see to the king's repayment of your gift." He took the man, still carrying his basket, to the palace gates. And there, just as the king had commanded, he made sure that every person who walked through the gates took a fig from the basket and threw it at the foolish man.

When the last fig had finally been aimed at the dazed fellow, the guards released him. Bruised and fruit-stained he returned home, clutching the empty basket. Immediately his wife began to scold him. "You dull-witted creature!" she cried. "I knew you would do something wrong!"

But the man only chuckled slowly as he rubbed his aching body. "It is your schemes that are dull-witted," he replied. "I myself thank the Lord for two things. I am thankful first that I brought figs in my basket, not coconuts; and second that I brought only a basketful, not a wagonful. If I had taken a wagonful of coconuts to the palace, I never would have come home alive!"

Questions

1 Why was Jacob willing to plant trees even though he was very old?

2 "It could always be worse." That is the conclusion of the foolish husband. Is he right? Give examples.

3 Was his wife nice? Was she ambitious? What does that mean?

4 Ambition can lead two ways; what are they? Is ambition good or bad?

28 The Death of Moses

Introduction

Moses, like all men, must die when God says so. If he does not die, he will be like a god himself. But Moses has served God faithfully, so when death comes to him, it is like the softest of sleeps.

Story

When Moses had brought the Israelites almost to Canaan, the Lord spoke to him, saying, "Go to the top of Mount Nebo, and look upon the countryside which I have promised to your people. For you may see the land from afar, but you shall not go into the land which I give to the children of Israel."

Moses climbed Mount Nebo. He looked down and saw mountains and plains and sparkling lakes, and the River Jordan winding its way across the land. Then, closing his eyes, he imagined how the land would look many generations later. He saw strong, healthy people, bringing a rich harvest from the fields; they sang and danced to celebrate a holiday, while around them happy children played. "O Lord," cried Moses, "let me live to enter the Promised Land, the land of my people!"

"No, Moses," God replied. "Ten times has your death been decreed in heaven. Now I make My vow once again: you shall not cross the Jordan."

"For forty years, O Lord, I served You faithfully," pleaded Moses. "Take back Your verdict. Let me live."

God's answer was firm. "The verdict cannot be changed. Like all mortals, you must die. So was it with your father, and your father's father, and all men before him, even back to Adam. Are any of them living now?"

"No," replied Moses.

"Your end must be like their end."

"But none of them ascended Mount Sinai and looked upon Your face as I did, O Lord," Moses implored. "My hands received the Law from You. Am I now to return to common dust?"

"That is the way of the world, Moses," God

replied. "You have been a mighty leader of your people, but now the time has come for Joshua, your student, to fill your place. The laws of the universe cannot be changed."

"But did You not change the law of the universe for Your people, the Israelites?" Moses persisted. "For them You divided the waters of the sea, and rained manna from heaven. Reverse this law as well, and let me live!"

"If you continued living and did not die, the people would worship you as a god," said the Lord.

"Then let me live as a little bird flitting about with the four winds, or as a little fish swimming in the Jordan. That would be enough; to be alive and part of the world," pleaded Moses.

But by now God's patience had worn thin. Sternly He said, "Moses, nothing you can say will change the decree of the Lord your God. You are about to die."

At last Moses realized that the time for his death had truly come. "Lord, I am ready now," he whispered.

God's voice became gentle. "Moses, My beloved, stretch out your feet."

Moses did so.

"Now close your eyes, Moses, My son."

Moses closed his eyes.

Then the Holy One descended from the highest reaches of heaven to take the soul of Moses. A sweet breeze passed over Moses' mouth. The Lord bent over Moses and plucked out his soul with a kiss. And Moses died, his lips still glowing with God's kiss.

Then there was weeping. The heavens and the earth wept. The angels of the Lord wept. The Israelites wept. Together they all wept. For there arose no Prophet in Israel like Moses.

Questions

1 Moses talked with God and God answered. Do you ever talk with God? Does He ever answer? Does He answer with words?

2 The Promised Land is a real place. Where is it today?

3 The Promised Land could also be a symbol. Then what would it be a symbol of?

4 Should God have let Moses live? Yes or no and why?